PRAYERS

of a DEDICATED

Teacher

FOURTH EDITION

PRAYERS

of a DEDICATED

Teacher

Cover Design by Kim Russell / Wahoo Designs
Page Layout by Bart Dawson

ISBN 1-58334-243-5

Printed in the United States of America

Table of Contents

Introduction

Because you're reading a book with the word "teacher" in its title, you probably *are* one. If so, congratulations! You are a member of one of the world's most important professions.

Henry Adams correctly observed, "A teacher affects eternity; he can never tell where his influence stops." Never have those words been more appropriate. We live in a difficult, fast-paced, temptation-filled world; more than ever, our young people need the direction and the leadership provided by teachers who know and love God.

This book contains devotional readings for Christians who teach. The text is divided into 31 chapters, one for each day of the month. During the next 31 days, please try this experiment: read a chapter each day. If you're already committed to a daily worship time, this book will enrich that experience—if not, the simple act of giving God a few minutes each morning will change the direction and the quality of your life.

Whether you teach graduate school or Sunday School, whether you lecture at seminary or at Vacation Bible School, you need and deserve a regularly scheduled conference with the *ultimate* Teacher. After all, you are God's emissary, a person charged with molding lives. God takes your teaching duties very seriously, and so should you.

Remember that God honors your profession just as surely as He offers His loving abundance to you and to your students. With God's help, you are destined to reshape eternity. It's a big job, but don't worry: You and God, working together, can handle it.

CHAPTER 1

Reshaping Eternity

*You will show me the path of life;
in Your presence is fullness of joy;
at Your right hand are pleasures forevermore.*

Psalm 16:11 NKJV

As a teacher, you work hard, and your hard work pays off in the lives of your students. Daniel Webster wrote, "If we work in marble, it will perish; if we work upon brass, time will efface it; if we rear temples, they will crumble into dust; but if we work upon immortal minds and instill in them just principles, we are then engraving upon tablets which no time will efface, but which will brighten and brighten to all eternity." These words remind us of the glorious opportunities that are available to those who teach.

May you, with God's help, touch the hearts and minds of your students and, by doing so, refashion *this* wonderful world . . . and *the next*. And as you teach, may you always be a shining example to your students of the changes that Christ can make in the lives of those who love Him.

If you want a surefire way to reshape the future,
here it is: find something *important* to say
to the next generation . . . and say it.

Marie T. Freeman

People who inspire others are those who see
invisible bridges at the end of dead-end streets.

Charles Swindoll

When God wants to accomplish something,
He calls dedicated men and women to
challenge His people and lead the way.

Warren Wiersbe

It may be that the day of judgment will
dawn tomorrow; in that case, we shall gladly
stop working for a better tomorrow.
But not before.

Dietrich Bonhoeffer

Wisdom is pleasing to you.
If you find it, you have hope for the future.

Proverbs 24:14 NCV

A Prayer for Today

You have given me an awesome responsibility,
Lord—You have allowed me to become
a teacher. As my students listen to my words
and observe my actions, may they see You,
Father, in all that I say and do.

Amen

CHAPTER 2

The Rewards (and Demands) of Teaching

Work hard so God can approve you.
Be a good worker, one who does not need
to be ashamed and who correctly explains
the word of truth.

2 Timothy 2:15 NLT

Being a teacher is not an easy job. The demands and pressures of the classroom, combined with late-night paper-grading marathons and lesson preparations, can leave even the most experienced teacher feeling overworked and under appreciated. Thankfully, teaching is not only a difficult job; it is also a highly rewarding one.

As a teacher, you have countless opportunities to do great things for God. So it's no surprise that the teaching profession is sometimes difficult. Reaching for great things usually requires work and lots of it, which is perfectly fine with God. After all, He knows that you're up to the task, and He has big plans for you *and* for your students. Very big plans . . .

We must trust as if it all depended on God and
work as if it all depended on us.

C. H. *Spurgeon*

I seem to have been led, little by little, toward
my work; and I believe that the same fact will
appear in the life of anyone who will cultivate
such powers as God has given him and
then go on, bravely, quietly, but persistently,
doing such work as comes to his hands.

Fanny Crosby

Ordinary work, which is what most of us do
most of the time, is ordained by God every bit
as much as is the extraordinary.

Elisabeth Elliot

"They that sow bountifully shall reap
also bountifully," is as true in spiritual things
as in material.

Lottie Moon

Then he said to his disciples,
"The harvest is plentiful but the workers are few.
Ask the Lord of the harvest, therefore,
to send out workers into his harvest field."

∽

Matthew 9:37 NIV

A Prayer for Today

Lord, I know that You desire a bountiful harvest
for all Your children. But, You have instructed
us that we must sow before we reap,
not after. Help me, Lord, to sow the seeds of
Your abundance everywhere I go. Let me be
diligent in all my undertakings and give me
patience to wait for Your harvest. In time, Lord,
let me reap the harvest that is found
in Your will for my life.

∽

Amen

CHAPTER 3

The Power of Prayer

*Ask and it shall be given to you;
seek and you shall find; knock and it shall be
opened to you. For every one who asks receives,
and he who seeks finds, and to him who knocks
it shall be opened.*

Matthew 7:7-8 NASB

"The power of prayer": these words are so familiar, yet sometimes we forget what they mean. Prayer is a powerful tool for communicating with our Creator; it is an opportunity to commune with the Giver of all things good. Prayer helps us find strength for today and hope for the future. Prayer is a tool we can use to help others. Prayer is not a thing to be taken lightly or to be used infrequently.

Is prayer an integral part of your life, or is it a hit-or-miss habit? Do you "pray without ceasing," or is your prayer life an afterthought? Do you regularly pray for your family, your friends, and your students . . . or do you bow your head only when others are watching?

The quality of your spiritual life will be in direct proportion to the quality of your prayer life. Prayer changes things, and it changes you. Today, instead of turning things over in your mind, turn them over to God in prayer. Instead of worrying about your next decision, ask God to lead the way. Don't limit your prayers to meals or to bedtime. Pray constantly about things great and small. God is listening, and He wants to hear from you now.

We can do nothing without prayer.
All things can be done by importunate prayer.
That is the teaching of Jesus Christ.

E. M. Bounds

The Scriptures teach that we can pray
effectively for one another and that such
a petition "availeth much." I believe God
honors and answers this kind of
intercessory prayer.

James Dobson

Lord, help us to have a listening heart that is
soft and teachable. Save us from being so filled
with ourselves that we can't hear you.
Give us the grace to both listen and obey
when you speak to us.

Jim Cymbala

Prayer may not get us what we want,
but it will teach us to want what we need.

Vance Havner

Therefore, let everyone who is godly pray to You.

Psalm 32:6 NASB

A Prayer for Today

Dear Lord, help me remember
the importance of prayer.
You *always* hear my prayers,
Father; let me always pray them!

Amen

CHAPTER 4

Using God's Gifts

Since we have gifts that differ according to the grace given to us, let each exercise them accordingly: if prophecy, according to the proportion of his faith; if service, in his serving; or he who teaches, in his teaching; or he who exhorts, in his exhortation; he who gives, with liberality; he who leads, with diligence; he who shows mercy, with cheerfulness.

Romans 12:6-8 NASB

All teachers possess special gifts—bestowed from the Father above—and you are no exception. Yet God's gifts are no guarantee of success; those gifts must be cultivated and nurtured; otherwise they diminish over time.

Perhaps you are one of those lucky teachers who has a *natural* gift for leading a class. But, even if you have the oratorical skills of Churchill and the mind of Einstein, you can *still* improve your teaching skills . . . and you should.

Today, accept this challenge: value the unique gift that God has given you—then, nourish your gift, make it grow, and share it with your students and with the world. After all, the best way to say "Thank You" for God's gift is, quite simply, to use it.

One thing taught large in the Holy Scriptures
is that while God gives His gifts freely,
He will require a strict accounting of them
at the end of the road. Each man is personally
responsible for his store, be it large or small, and
will be required to explain his use of it
before the judgment seat of Christ.

A. W. Tozer

You are the only person on earth
who can use your ability.

Zig Ziglar

In the great orchestra we call life, you have
an instrument and a song, and you owe it
to God to play them both sublimely.

Max Lucado

God often reveals His direction for our lives
through the way He made us . . .
with a certain personality and unique skills.

Bill Hybels

I remind you to fan into flame the gift of God.

2 Timothy 1:6 NIV

A Prayer for Today

Dear Lord, let me use my gifts,
and let me help my students discover theirs.
Your gifts are priceless and eternal.
May we, Your children, use them to the glory
of Your kingdom, today and forever.

Amen

CHAPTER 5

The Power of a Teacher's Example

Therefore, get your minds ready for action,
being self-disciplined, and set your hope completely
on the grace to be brought to you at the revelation
of Jesus Christ. As obedient children, do not be
conformed to the desires of your former ignorance
but, as the One who called you is holy, you also are
to be holy in all your conduct.

1 Peter 1:13-15 HCSB

Teachers serve as powerful examples to their students. Wise teachers understand that while words often fall upon closed ears, actions do not. And, godly teachers behave accordingly.

Life is a series of decisions and choices. Each day, we make countless decisions that can bring us closer to God . . . or not. When we live according to God's commandments, we earn for ourselves the abundance and peace that He intends for our lives. But, when we turn our backs upon God by disobeying Him, we bring needless suffering upon ourselves and our families.

Do you seek God's peace and His blessings? Then obey Him. When you're faced with a difficult choice or a powerful temptation, seek God's counsel and trust the counsel He gives. Invite God into your heart and live according to His commandments. When you do, you will be blessed—and your example will serve as a powerful blessing to your students, to your family, and to the world.

More depends on my walk than my talk.

D. L. Moody

There may be no trumpet sound or loud applause when we make a right decision, just a calm sense of resolution and peace.

Gloria Gaither

What you do reveals what you believe about God, regardless of what you say. When God reveals what He has purposed you to do, you face a crisis—a decision time. God and the world can tell from your response what you really believe about God.

Henry Blackaby

If the Spirit of God has transformed you within, you will exhibit Divine characteristics in your life, not good human characteristics. God's life in us expresses itself as God's life, not as a human life trying to be godly.

Oswald Chambers

*And we pray this in order that you may live
a life worthy of the Lord and may please him
in every way: bearing fruit in every good work,
growing in the knowledge of God.*

❧

Colossians 1:10 NIV

A Prayer for Today

Lord, because I am a teacher, I am a role model
to my students. I pray that my actions will
always be consistent with my beliefs. I know
that my deeds speak more loudly than my
words. May every step that I take reflect
Your truth and love, and may others be drawn
to You because of my words and my deeds.

❧

Amen

CHAPTER 6

Change

There is a time for everything,
and a season for every activity under heaven.

Ecclesiastes 3:1 NIV

Our world is in a state of constant change, and so, too, is the teaching profession. At times, the world seems to be trembling beneath our feet. But we can be comforted in the knowledge that our Heavenly Father is the rock that cannot be shaken. His Word promises, "I am the LORD, I do not change" (Malachi 3:6 NKJV).

Every day that we live, we mortals encounter a multitude of changes—some good, some not so good. And on occasion, all of us must endure life-changing personal losses that leave us breathless. When we do, our loving Heavenly Father stands ready to protect us, to comfort us, to guide us, and, in time, to heal us.

Are you facing difficult circumstances or unwelcome changes? If so, please remember that God is far bigger than any problem you may face. So, instead of worrying about life's inevitable challenges, put your faith in the Father and His only begotten Son: "Jesus Christ is the same yesterday, today, and forever" (Hebrews 13:8 HCSB). And rest assured: It is precisely because your Savior does not change that you can face your challenges with courage for this day and hope for the future.

God wants to change our lives—and He will,
as we open our hearts to Him.

Billy Graham

Conditions are always changing; therefore,
I must not be dependent upon conditions.
What matters supremely is my soul
and my relationship to God.

Corrie ten Boom

With God, it isn't who you were that matters;
it's who you are becoming.

Liz Curtis Higgs

Sometimes your medicine bottle says,
"Shake well before using." That is what God
has to do with some of his people.
He has to shake them well before
they are usable.

Vance Havner

*Therefore do not worry about tomorrow,
for tomorrow will worry about itself.
Each day has enough trouble of its own.*

◦

Matthew 6:34 NIV

A Prayer for Today

Dear Lord, our world changes, but You are
unchanging. When I face challenges that leave
me discouraged or fearful, I will turn to You
for strength and assurance. Let my trust
in You—like Your love for me—
be unchanging and everlasting.

◦

Amen

CHAPTER 7

Success . . .
According
to God

Success, success to you, and success to those who help you, for your God will help you . . . .
1 Chronicles 12:18 NIV

H ow do you define success? Do you define it as the accumulation of material possessions or the adulation of your co-workers? If so, you need to reorder your priorities. Genuine success has little to do with fame or fortune; it has everything to do with God's gift of love and His promise of salvation.

If you have allowed Christ to reign in your heart, you are already a towering success in the eyes of God, but there is still more that you can do. Your task—as a believer who has been touched by the Creator's grace—is to accept the spiritual abundance and peace that He offers through the person of His Son. Then, you can share the healing message of God's love and His abundance with a world that desperately needs both. When you do, you have reached the pinnacle of success.

Success and happiness are not destinations.
They are exciting, never-ending journeys.

Zig Ziglar

Often, attitude is the only difference
between success and failure.

John Maxwell

We, as believers, must allow God to define
success. And, when we do, God blesses us with
His love and His grace.

Jim Gallery

Victory is the result of Christ's life lived out in
the believer. It is important to see that victory,
not defeat, is God's purpose for His children.

Corrie ten Boom

*Let us not become weary in doing good,
for at the proper time we will reap
a harvest if we do not give up.*

Galatians 6:9 NIV

A Prayer for Today

Dear Lord, You have given me another day of
life. Today, let me be successful in *Your* eyes.
And, help me, Father, see more clearly the path
You have chosen for me. I praise You, Lord,
for my life and for the friends, family members,
and students who make it rich. Enable me to
live each moment to the fullest as
I give thanks for Your creation, for Your love,
and for Your Son.

Amen

My Thoughts & Prayers
from This Week

_____

_____

_____

_____

_____

_____

_____

_____

_____

_____

_____

_____

_____

_____

_____

_____

_____

_____

_____

_____

_____

_____

_____

_____

My Thoughts & Prayers
for Next Week

CHAPTER 8

Teaching the Art of Responsible Living

Now he who plants and he who waters are one,
and each one will receive his own reward according
to his own labor.

1 Corinthians 3:8 NKJV

As teachers, we find ourselves preaching the gospel of responsible behavior. Unfortunately, our sermons often fall upon deaf ears. Despite warnings to the contrary, young people sometimes behave inappropriately; they sometimes behave impulsively; they sometimes behave foolishly. Why? Because they are human beings and because they are young.

Our task—as concerned adults who seek to impart the importance of responsible behavior—is to keep teaching the art of responsible living by word *and* by example. And the greatest of these, of course, is example.

Action springs not from thought,
but from a readiness for responsibility.

Dietrich Bonhoeffer

Jesus knows one of the greatest barriers to
our faith is often our unwillingness to be
made whole—our unwillingness to accept
responsibility—our unwillingness
to live without excuse for our
spiritual smallness and immaturity.

Anne Graham Lotz

God's sovereignty is a reality,
and man's responsibility is a reality too.

J. I. Packer

The most important work of the gospel is done
directly by citizens living out their biblical
responsibility in their everyday circumstances.

Chuck Colson

*So then each of us shall give account
of himself to God.*

Romans 14:12 NKJV

A Prayer for Today

Dear Lord, let me live responsibly, and let me
demonstrate the art of responsible living to my
students, to my friends, and to my family. It is
so much easier *to speak* of the righteous life than
it is *to live it.* Let me live righteously, and let my
actions be consistent with my beliefs.
And finally, Father, let every step that I take
reflect Your truth and Your love.

Amen

CHAPTER 9

Choices That Are Pleasing to God

*I have set before you life and death, blessings
and curses. Now choose life, so that you
and your children may live and that you may love
the LORD your God, listen to his voice,
and hold fast to him.*

Deuteronomy 30:19-20 NIV

L ife is a series of choices. From the instant we wake in the morning until the moment we nod off to sleep at night, we make countless decisions: decisions about the things we do, decisions about the words we speak, and decisions about the thoughts we choose to think. Simply put, the quality of those decisions determines the quality of our lives.

As believers who have been saved by a loving and merciful God, we have every reason to make wise choices. Yet sometimes, amid the inevitable hustle and bustle of life here on earth, we allow ourselves to behave in ways that we know are displeasing to God. When we do, we forfeit— albeit temporarily—the joy and the peace that we might otherwise experience through Him.

As you consider the next step in your life's journey—whether inside or outside the classroom—take time to consider how many things in this life you can control: your thoughts, your words, your priorities, and your actions, for starters. And then, if you sincerely want to discover God's purpose for your life, make choices that are pleasing to Him. He deserves no less . . . and neither do you.

I do not know how the Spirit of Christ performs
it, but He brings us choices through which
we constantly change, fresh and new,
into His likeness.

Joni Eareckson Tada

Faith is not a feeling; it is action.
It is a willed choice.

Elisabeth Elliot

Every time you make a choice, you are turning
the central part of you, the part that chooses,
into something a little different
from what it was before.

C. S. Lewis

Commitment to His lordship on Easter,
at revivals, or even every Sunday is not enough.
We must choose this day—and every day—
whom we will serve. This deliberate act of
the will is the inevitable choice between
habitual fellowship and habitual failure.

Beth Moore

Therefore, since we have this ministry,
as we received mercy, we do not lose heart,
but we have renounced the things hidden because
of shame, not walking in craftiness or adulterating
the word of God, but by the manifestation
of truth commending ourselves to every man's
conscience in the sight of God.

~

2 Corinthians 4:1-2 NASB

A Prayer for Today

Dear Lord, help me to make choices
that are pleasing to You. Help me to be honest,
patient, and kind. And above all, help me
to follow the teachings of Jesus, not just today,
but every day of my life.

~

Amen

CHAPTER 10

The Words That We Speak

A wise man's heart guides his mouth,
and his lips promote instruction.

Proverbs 16:23 NIV

Think . . . pause . . . then speak: How wise is the teacher who can communicate in this way. But occasionally, amid the pressures of the school day, even the most considerate teacher may speak first and think next . . . with unfortunate results.

God's Word reminds us that "Reckless words pierce like a sword, but the tongue of the wise brings healing" (Proverbs 12:18 NIV). If we seek to be a source of encouragement to our students, to our peers, and to our families, then we must measure our words carefully. Words are important: they can hurt or heal. Words can uplift us or discourage us, and reckless words, spoken in haste, cannot be erased.

Today, seek to encourage all who cross your path. Measure your words carefully. Speak wisely, not impulsively. Use words of kindness and praise, not words of anger or derision. Remember that you have the power to heal others or to injure them, to lift others up or to hold them back. When you lift them up, your wisdom will bring healing and comfort to a classroom, *and* a world, that need both.

Part of good communication is listening
with the eyes as well as with the ears.

Josh McDowell

We should ask ourselves three things
before we speak: Is it true?
Is it kind? Does it glorify God?

Billy Graham

When you talk, choose the very same words
that you would use if Jesus were looking over
your shoulder. Because He is.

Marie T. Freeman

The great test of a man's character is his tongue.

Oswald Chambers

*The righteous man walks in his integrity;
his children are blessed after him.*

∾

Proverbs 20:7 NKJV

A Prayer for Today

Lord, You have warned me that I will be
judged by the words I speak. And, You have
commanded me to choose my words carefully
so that I might be a source of encouragement
and hope to all whom I meet. Keep me mindful,
Lord, that I have influence on many people;
make me an influence for good. And, may
the words that I speak today be worthy
of the One who has saved me forever.

∾

Amen

CHAPTER 11

The Value
of Education

Commit yourself to instruction;
attune your ears to hear words of knowledge.

Proverbs 23:12 NLT

Teachers understand the value of education. Students often do not. Thus the first lesson that a good teacher must often teach is the importance of education.

Education is the tool by which we come to know and appreciate the world in which we live. It is the shining light that snuffs out the darkness of ignorance and poverty. Education is freedom just as surely as ignorance is a form of bondage. Education is not a luxury; it is a necessity and a powerful tool for good in this world.

Knowledge can be found in textbooks. Wisdom, on the other hand, is found in God's Holy Word and in the carefully chosen words of loving parents and thoughtful teachers. When we give our children the gift of knowledge, we do them a wonderful service. But, when we share the gift of wisdom, we offer a timeless treasure that surpasses knowledge and reshapes eternity.

Education without religion, as useful as it is,
seems rather to make a man a more clever devil.

C. S. Lewis

Education is useless without the Bible.

Noah Webster

Crafty men condemn studies; simple men
admire them, and wise men use them.

Francis Bacon

I am much afraid that the schools and
universities will prove to be the great gates
to hell unless they diligently labor to explain
the Holy Scriptures and engrave them upon
the hearts of youth. I advise no one to send
their child where the Scriptures do not reign
paramount. Every institution that does not
unceasingly occupy its students with
the Word of God must become corrupt.

Martin Luther

Give instruction to a wise man,
and he will be still wiser;
Teach a just man,
and he will increase in learning.

Proverbs 9:9 NKJV

A Prayer for Today

Lord, You are my Teacher. Help me to be
a student of Your Word and a servant of
Your will. Let me live by the truth
You reveal; let me trust in the wisdom of
Your commandments; and,
let me teach others the glory of Your ways.

Amen

CHAPTER 12

Switching to Plan B

But one thing I do: Forgetting what is behind
and straining toward what is ahead, I press on
toward the goal to win the prize for which
God has called me heavenward in Christ Jesus.

Philippians 3:13-14 NIV

N o lesson plan is perfect; sometimes, savvy teachers must make mid-course corrections during class . . . or else! And so it is with life: Sometimes, we must make major modifications in our hopes, dreams, goals, and plans . . . *or else*.

Some of our most important dreams are the ones we abandon. Some of our most important goals are the ones we don't attain. Sometimes, our most important journeys are the ones that we take to the winding conclusion of what seems to be a dead end street. Thankfully, with God there are no dead ends; there are only opportunities to learn, to yield, to trust, to serve, and to grow.

The next time you experience one of life's inevitable disappointments, don't despair and don't be afraid to try "Plan B." Consider every setback an opportunity to choose a different, more appropriate path. Have faith that God may indeed be leading you in an entirely different direction, a direction of *His* choosing. And as you take your next step, remember that what looks like a dead end to you may, in fact, be the fast lane according to God.

God is the only goal worthy of man's efforts;
the fitting end of human existence is
a loving union with God.

St. Augustine

What you get by reaching your goals is
not nearly as important as what you
become by reaching them.

Zig Ziglar

God's goal is not to make you happy.
It is to make you his.

Max Lucado

When our plans are interrupted, his are not.
His plans are proceeding exactly as scheduled,
moving us always—including those minutes
or hours or years which seem most useless
or wasted or unendurable—
toward the goal of true maturity.

Elisabeth Elliot

So we make it our goal to please him . . .

❦

2 Corinthians 5:9 NIV

A Prayer for Today

Dear Lord, You have a goal for my life.
Let me discover it and live it. And, let me help
others seek Your will. Today, I will seek the
wisdom of Your perfect plan, Father,
knowing that when I trust in You,
I am eternally blessed.

❦

Amen

CHAPTER 13

The Opportunity to Teach

Make the most of every opportunity.

Colossians 4:5 NIV

Are you genuinely excited about the opportunity of being a teacher? Are you enthusiastic about the opportunities of today and thrilled by the possibilities of tomorrow? Do you confidently expect God to lead you and your students to a place of abundance, peace, and joy? And, when your days on earth are over, do you expect to receive the priceless gift of eternal life? If you trust God's promises, and if you have welcomed God's Son into your heart, then you believe that your future is intensely and eternally bright.

Today, as you prepare to meet your duties inside *and* outside the classroom, pause to consider God's promises. And then think for a moment about the wonderful future that awaits all believers, including you. God has promised that your future is secure. Trust that promise, and celebrate the life of abundance and eternal joy that is now yours through Christ.

Life is a glorious opportunity.

Billy Graham

A wise man makes more opportunities
than he finds.

Francis Bacon

God surrounds you with opportunity.
You and I are free in Jesus Christ,
not to do whatever we want,
but to be all that God wants us to be.

Warren Wiersbe

Great opportunities often disguise
themselves in small tasks.

Rick Warren

*Let us not lose heart in doing good, for in
due time we shall reap if we do not grow weary.
So then, while we have opportunity,
let us do good to all men, and especially
to those who are of the household of the faith.*

∽

Galatians 6:9-10 NASB

A Prayer for Today

Lord, thank You for the opportunity to teach.
When I am weary, give me strength. When I am
frustrated, give me patience. And, let my words
and deeds always demonstrate to that roomful
of wonderful students the love that
I feel for them . . . and for You.

∽

Amen

CHAPTER 14

Integrity

*Till I die I will not remove mine integrity from me.
My righteousness I hold fast, and will not let it go:
my heart shall not reproach me so long as I live.*

Job 27:5-6 KJV

From the time we are children, we are taught that honesty is the best policy. And, in the classroom, we instruct our students that honesty is also *the school's* policy. But, honesty is not just the best policy or the school's policy, it is also *God's* policy. If we are to be servants worthy of His holy blessings, we must remember that truth is not just the best way; it is God's way. May we, as teachers, preach truth and practice it . . . but not necessarily in that order.

Charles Swindoll correctly observed, "Nothing speaks louder or more powerfully than a life of integrity." Dedicated teachers agree. Integrity is built slowly over a lifetime. It is a precious thing—difficult to build but easy to tear down. As believers in Christ, we must seek to live each day with discipline, honesty, and faith—and we must encourage our students to do likewise.

Living a life of integrity isn't always the easiest way, but it is always the right way. And God clearly intends that it should be *our* way, too.

God never called us to naïveté. He called us
to integrity . . . . The biblical concept
of integrity emphasizes mature innocence
not childlike ignorance.

Beth Moore

Integrity is the glue that holds our way of life
together. We must constantly strive to keep our
integrity intact. When wealth is lost, nothing
is lost; when health is lost, something is lost;
when character is lost, all is lost.

Billy Graham

Image is what people think we are;
integrity is what we really are.

John Maxwell

Integrity of heart is indispensable.

John Calvin

The godly walk with integrity;
blessed are their children after them.

Proverbs 20:7 NLT

A Prayer for Today

Lord, You are my Father in Heaven.
You search my heart and know me far better
than I know myself. May I be Your worthy
servant, and may I live according to
Your commandments. Let me be a person of
integrity, Lord, and let my words
and deeds be a testimony to You,
today and always.

Amen

My Thoughts & Prayers
from This Week

My Thoughts & Prayers
for Next Week

_____

_____

_____

_____

_____

_____

_____

_____

_____

_____

_____

_____

_____

_____

_____

_____

_____

_____

_____

_____

_____

_____

_____

CHAPTER 15

Dealing with Difficult People

You have heard it said, "Love your neighbor
and hate your enemy." But I tell you:
Love your enemies and pray for those who
persecute you, that you may be sons of
your Father in heaven.

Matthew 5:43-45 NIV

All of us can be grumpy, hardheaded, and difficult to deal with at times. And as teachers, we must, from time to time, encounter out-of-sorts parents or their out-of-sorts offspring. When you have occasion to deal with difficult people (and you will), the following tips should help:

1. **Do Make Sure That You're Not the One Being Difficult**: Perhaps the problems that concern you have their origin, at least partially, within your own heart. If so, fix yourself first. (Philippians 2:3)

2. **Don't Try to Change the Other Person**: Unless the person you're trying to change is a young child, and unless you are that child's parent or guardian, don't try to change him or her. Why? Because teenagers and adults change when they want to, not when you want them to. (Proverbs 10:14)

3. **Do Insist Upon Logical Consequences to Irresponsible Behavior**: When you protect other people from the consequences of their misbehavior, you're doing those folks a profound disservice. Most people don't learn new behaviors until the old behaviors stop

working, so don't be an enabler. (Hebrews 12:5-6)

4. **Don't Allow Yourself to Become Caught Up in the Other Person's Emotional Outbursts**: If someone is ranting, raving, or worse, you have the right to excuse yourself and leave. Remember: emotions are highly contagious, so if the other person is angry, you will soon become angry, too. Instead of adding your own emotional energy to the outburst, you should make the conscious effort to remain calm—and part of remaining calm may be leaving the scene. (Proverbs 22:24-25)

And finally, when you've finished dealing with that difficult person, do your best to forget about the confrontation. Everybody's human, and everybody needs forgiveness. And that includes, parents, students, and—on rare occasions—teachers, too.

We are all fallen creatures and
all very hard to live with.

C. S. Lewis

*Do not answer a fool according to his folly,
or you will be like him yourself.*

Proverbs 26:4 NIV

A Prayer for Today

Heavenly Father, give me patience.
Let me live according to Your plan and
according to Your timetable. When I am
hurried, slow me down. When I become
impatient with others, give me empathy.
When I am frustrated by the demands of
the day, give me peace. Today, let me be
a patient Christian, Dear Lord,
as I trust in You and in Your master plan
for my life.

Amen

CHAPTER 16

Forgiveness

Be kind to each other, tenderhearted,
forgiving one another,
just as God through Christ has forgiven you.

Ephesians 4:32 NLT

Forgiveness is God's commandment, but oh how difficult a commandment it can be to follow. Being frail, fallible, imperfect human beings, we are quick to anger, quick to blame, slow to forgive, and even slower to forget. No matter. Forgiveness, although difficult, is God's way.

Teachers, having been placed in positions of leadership, serve as important role models to their students. As such, teachers must be models of forgiveness, both inside the classroom and out. We must, on occasion, forgive those who have injured us; to do otherwise is to disobey God.

If there exists even one person, alive or dead, whom you have not forgiven (and that includes yourself), follow God's commandment and His will for your life: forgive. Hatred and bitterness and regret are not part of God's plan for your life. Forgiveness is.

Forgiveness is God's command.

Martin Luther

I believe that forgiveness can become
a continuing cycle: because God forgives us,
we're to forgive others; because we forgive
others, God forgives us.
Scripture presents both parts of the cycle.

Shirley Dobson

Forgiveness is contagious.
First you forgive them, and pretty soon,
they'll forgive you, too.

Marie T. Freeman

Forgiveness is the final form of love.

Reinhold Niebuhr

*Be kind to each other, tenderhearted,
forgiving one another, just as God through
Christ has forgiven you.*

❧

Ephesians 4:32 NLT

A Prayer for Today

Dear Lord, Your ability to forgive is limitless;
mine is not. Keep me mindful of
Your commandment to forgive others—
and *to keep* forgiving them—
just as I have been forgiven by You.

❧

Amen

CHAPTER 17

The Power of Encouragement

Encourage each other. Live in harmony and peace.
Then the God of love and peace will be with you.

2 Corinthians 13:11 NLT

In the classroom, we encounter a specific category of people who desperately need our encouraging words: those people are called students—*all* students. And, as dedicated teachers, we must find creative ways to encourage them.

Today's world can be a difficult and uncertain place, especially for young people. Many of our students are in desperate need of a smile or an encouraging word, and since we don't always know who needs our help, the best strategy is to encourage all those who cross our paths. So today, as you address a classroom, be an enthusiastic booster and a proponent of possibilities. Who knows? Your encouraging words might just change someone's day . . . or someone's life.

Make it a rule, and pray to God to help you
to keep it, never to lie down at night without
being able to say: "I have made at least one
human being a little wiser, a little happier,
or a little better this day."

Charles Kingsley

God grant that we may not hinder those who
are battling their way slowly into the light.

Oswald Chambers

How many people stop because so few say,
"Go!"

Charles Swindoll

Isn't it funny the way some combinations of
words can give you—almost apart from
their meaning—a thrill like music?

C. S. Lewis

> *Do not let any unwholesome talk come
> out of your mouths, but only what is helpful
> for building others up according to their needs,
> that it may benefit those who listen.*
>
> ❧
>
> Ephesians 4:29 NIV

A Prayer for Today

Dear Father, make me an encouraging teacher.
Just as You have lifted me up, let me also lift
up my students in the spirit of encouragement
and hope. Today, let me help my students find
the strength and the courage to use their gifts
according to Your master plan.

❧

Amen

CHAPTER 18

Enthusiasm

Do your work with enthusiasm.
Work as if you were serving the Lord,
not as if you were serving only men and women.

Ephesians 6:7 NCV

Jesus promises that we can have joy and abundance through Him. Of course, teaching should be a joyful experience, but every teacher knows that some days are so busy and so hurried that abundance seems a distant promise. It is not. Every day, we can claim the spiritual abundance that God promises for our lives. When we do so, we reap bountiful rewards for our families, our students, and ourselves.

Are you an enthusiastic, optimistic, joyful teacher? You should be. Are you a living, breathing example of the spiritual abundance that Christ offers His believers? Hopefully, you are. Your students need positive role models who clearly demonstrate the transforming power of Christ's love. By sharing the joy that you feel in your heart, you become a powerful force for good in a world that desperately needs positive influences such as yours.

Catch on fire with enthusiasm and
people will come for miles to watch you burn.

John Wesley

When we wholeheartedly commit ourselves
to God, there is nothing mediocre or
run-of-the-mill about us.
To live for Christ is to be passionate
about our Lord and about our lives.

Jim Gallery

Wherever you are, be all there.
Live to the hilt every situation you believe to be
the will of God.

Jim Elliot

We act as though comfort and luxury were
the chief requirements of life, when all we need
to make us really happy is something
to be enthusiastic about.

Charles Kingsley

*Whatever you do, work at it with all your heart,
as working for the Lord, not for men.*

Colossians 3:23 NIV

A Prayer for Today

Dear Lord, You can make all things new.
I am a new creature in Christ Jesus,
and when I fall short in my commitment,
You can renew my effort and my enthusiasm.
When I am weak or worried, restore my
strength, Lord, for my own sake
and for the sake of Your kingdom.

Amen

CHAPTER 19

Hope for the Future

Wisdom is pleasing to you.
If you find it, you have hope for the future.
Proverbs 24:14 NCV

As you consider God's unfolding plans for your life, you will undoubtedly look to the future . . . after all, the future is where those plans will take place. But sometimes, the future may seem foreboding indeed.

In these uncertain times, it's easy to lose faith in the possibility of a better tomorrow . . . but it's wrong. God instructs us to trust His wisdom, His plan, and His love. When we do so, the future becomes a glorious opportunity to help others, to praise our Creator, and to share God's Good News.

Do you have faith in the ultimate goodness of God's plan? You should. And, do you have faith in the abundant opportunities that await your students? Hopefully, you do. After all, the confidence that you display in your students can be contagious: Your belief in them can have a profound impact on the way they view themselves and their world.

Today, as you stand before your classroom, help your students face the future with optimism, hope, and self-confidence. After all, even in these uncertain times, God still has the last word. And His love endures to all generations, including this one.

Do not limit the limitless God!
With Him, face the future unafraid
because you are never alone.

Mrs. Charles E. Cowman

For Christians who believe God's promises,
the future is actually too bright to comprehend.

Marie T. Freeman

Like little children on Christmas Eve,
we know that lovely surprises are in the making.
We can't see them. We have simply been told,
and we believe. *Tomorrow we shall see.*

Elisabeth Elliot

Take courage. We walk in the wilderness today
and in the Promised Land tomorrow.

D. L. Moody

For I know the thoughts that I think toward you,
says the Lord, thoughts of peace and not of evil,
to give you a future and a hope. Then you will
call upon Me and go and pray to Me,
and I will listen to you.

∾

Jeremiah 29:11-12 NKJV

A Prayer for Today

Dear Lord, I will place my hope in You.
If I become discouraged, I will turn to You.
If I am afraid, I will seek strength in You.
In every aspect of my life, I will trust You.
You are my Father, and I will place my hope,
my trust, and my faith in You.

∾

Amen

CHAPTER 20

A Special Responsibility

In every way be an example of
doing good deeds. When you teach,
do it with honesty and seriousness.

Titus 2:7 NCV

God has a plan for all of us, students and teachers alike. As a teacher, you bear a special responsibility for training the students who are entrusted to your care. Because of your position as a guide and mentor, you must be especially careful to seek God's will and to follow it.

God will not force His will upon you. To the contrary, He has given you the free will to follow His commandments . . . or not. If you stray from those commandments, you invite bitter consequences. But, when you choose to follow Him by genuinely and humbly seeking His will, God will touch your heart and lead you on the path of His choosing.

Being a godly teacher in today's difficult world requires insight, discipline, patience, and prayer. May you, with God's help, touch the hearts and minds of your students and, in doing so, refashion this wonderful world . . . and the next.

If you want to be a teacher, remember that
you're just as likely to teach who you are as
you are to teach what you know.

Marie T. Freeman

Their little minds had a thousand hands
reaching and grabbing for everything they could
see (not unlike their physical hands).
A parent-teacher's job is to guide as much as
possible what the hands of their minds
grab and store.

Beth Moore

Let us look upon our children; let us love them
and train them as children of the covenant
and children of the promise.
These are the children of God.

Andrew Murray

We must go out and live among them,
manifesting the gentle, loving spirit of our Lord.
We need to make friends before we can
hope to make converts.

Lottie Moon

Wise people's minds tell them what to say,
and that helps them be better teachers.

Proverbs 16:23 NCV

A Prayer for Today

Dear Lord, there is so much to teach and
so little time. Let me share Your wisdom with
my students, with my family, and with
the world. And, let my love for You be
evident in the lessons that I teach and
the life that I live.

Amen

CHAPTER 21

The Quest for Knowledge and Wisdom

For this very reason, make every effort to supplement your faith with goodness, goodness with knowledge, knowledge with self-control, self-control with endurance, endurance with godliness.

2 Peter 1:5-6 HCSB

I f we are to grow as Christians and as teachers, we need both knowledge and wisdom. Knowledge is found in textbooks. Wisdom, on the other hand, is found in God's Holy Word and in the carefully-chosen words of loving parents, family members, and friends.

Wisdom is not accumulated overnight. It is like a savings account that accrues slowly over time, and the person who consistently adds to his account will eventually accumulate a great sum. The secret to success is consistency.

Do you seek wisdom for yourself and for your students? Then keep learning and keep motivating them to do likewise. The ultimate source of wisdom, of course, is—first and foremost—the Word of God. When you begin a daily study of God's Word and live according to His commandments, you will become wise . . . and so, in time, will your students.

Knowledge is power.

Francis Bacon

The doorstep to the temple of wisdom is
a knowledge of our own ignorance.

C.H. Spurgeon

All the wisdom you want is comprised
in one book, the Bible.

John Wesley

God Himself is what enlightens understanding
about everything else in life.
Knowledge about any subject is fragmentary
without the enlightenment that comes
from His relationship to it.

Beth Moore

*The fear of the LORD is the beginning of knowledge,
but fools despise wisdom and discipline.*

Proverbs 1:7 NIV

A Prayer for Today

Dear Lord, I have lots to learn.
Help me to watch, to listen, to think,
and to learn, every day of my life.

Amen

My Thoughts & Prayers
from This Week

My Thoughts & Prayers
for Next Week

CHAPTER 22

Dreaming Big Dreams

Where there is no vision, the people perish . . . .
Proverbs 29:18 KJV

Are you willing to entertain the possibility that God has big plans in store for you as well as for your students? Hopefully so. Yet sometimes, especially if you've recently experienced a life-altering disappointment, you may find it difficult to envision the possibility of a brighter future. If so, it's time to stop placing limitations upon yourself, upon your students, and upon God.

Your Heavenly Father created you with unique gifts and untapped talents; your job is to tap them. When you do, you'll begin to feel an increasing sense of confidence in yourself *and* in your future. Then, you can share that confidence with your students, with your family, and with your friends.

It takes courage to dream big dreams. You will discover that courage when you do three things: accept the past, trust God to handle the future, and make the most of the time He has given you today.

Nothing is too difficult for God, and no dreams are too big for Him—not even yours. So start living—and dreaming—accordingly.

You cannot out-dream God.

John Eldredge

The future lies all before us. Shall it only be
a slight advance upon what we usually do?
Ought it not to be a bound, a leap forward
to altitudes of endeavor and
success undreamed of before?

Annie Armstrong

Sometimes our dreams were so big
that it took two people to dream them.

Marie T. Freeman

Down through the centuries in times of trouble
and trial, God has brought courage to the hearts
of those who love Him. The Bible is filled with
assurances of God's help and comfort in every
kind of trouble which might cause fears to arise
in the human heart. You can look ahead with
promise, hope, and joy.

Billy Graham

*We can make our plans,
but the LORD determines our steps.*

Proverbs 16:9 NLT

A Prayer for Today

Dear Lord, give me the courage to dream and
the wisdom to help my students do likewise.
When I am worried or weary, give me strength
for today and hope for tomorrow.
Keep me mindful of Your miraculous power,
Your infinite love, and Your eternal salvation.

Amen

CHAPTER 23

God's Word

Man shall not live by bread alone,
but by every word that proceeds
from the mouth of God.

Matthew 4:4 NKJV

Is God's Word a lamp that guides your behavior in the classroom and beyond? Is God's Word your indispensable compass for everyday living, or is it relegated to Sunday morning services? Do you read the Bible faithfully or sporadically? The answer to these questions will determine the direction of your thoughts, the direction of your day, and the direction of your life.

God's Word is unlike any other book. The Bible is a roadmap for life here on earth and for life eternal. As Christians, we are called upon to study God's Holy Word, to trust its promises, to follow its commandments, and to share its Good News with the world.

As believers, we must study the Bible and meditate upon its meaning for our lives. Otherwise, we deprive ourselves of a priceless gift from our Creator. God's Holy Word is, indeed, a transforming, life-changing, one-of-a-kind treasure. And, a passing acquaintance with the Good Book is insufficient for Christians who seek to obey God's Word and to understand His will. After all, neither man nor woman should live by bread alone . . . .

Walking in faith brings you to
the Word of God.
There you will be healed, cleansed, fed,
nurtured, equipped, and matured.

Kay Arthur

If you believe what you like in the Gospel and
reject what you don't like,
it is not the Gospel you believe, but yourself.

St. Augustine

If we are not continually fed with God's Word,
we will starve spiritually.

Stormie Omartian

For the word of God is living and effective and sharper than any two-edged sword, penetrating as far as to divide soul, spirit, joints, and marrow; it is a judge of the ideas and thoughts of the heart.

Hebrews 4:12 HCSB

A Prayer for Today

Heavenly Father, Your Holy Word is a light unto the world; let me study it, trust it, and share it with all who cross my path. In all that I do, help me be a worthy witness for You as I share the Good News of Your perfect Son and Your perfect Word.

Amen

CHAPTER 24

Helping Students Mature

*Train up a child in the way he should go,
and when he is old he will not depart from it.*

Proverbs 22:6 NKJV

I f only our students would behave maturely and responsibly, teaching would be a breeze. But, here in the real world, young people don't grow into mature adults overnight. So what's a teacher to do? Be patient, be understanding, and be demanding.

God's Word teaches us the value of hard work and discipline. In his second letter to the Thessalonians, Paul warns, ". . . if any would not work, neither should he eat" (3:10 KJV). And the Book of Proverbs proclaims, "One who is slack in his work is brother to one who destroys" (18:9 NIV). In short, God has created a world in which diligence is rewarded, but sloth is not.

Teachers who allow undisciplined behavior to go unchecked are doing a disservice to their students. God does not reward laziness, nor does He praise misbehavior, and neither should we.

No matter what we are going through,
no matter how long the waiting for answers,
of one thing we may be sure. God is faithful.
He keeps His promises. What He starts,
He finishes . . . including His perfect work in us.

Gloria Gaither

The maturity of a Christian experience cannot
be reached in a moment, but is the result of
the work of God's Holy Spirit, who,
by His energizing and transforming power,
causes us to grow up into Christ in all things.

Hannah Whitall Smith

The wonderful thing about God's schoolroom is
that we get to grade our own papers.
You see, He doesn't test us so *He* can learn how
well we're doing. He tests us so *we* can
discover how well we're doing.

Charles Swindoll

> *But grow in grace, and in the knowledge of*
> *our Lord and Saviour Jesus Christ . . . .*
>
> ❧
>
> 2 Peter 3:18 KJV

A Prayer for Today

Lord, make me a wise counselor to those
whom I teach. Make me a worthy mentor
and a godly example to my students.
Let me lead them in the ways of wisdom,
discipline, and righteousness by the words that
I speak and the way that I live my life.

❧

Amen

CHAPTER 25

Your Priorities . . . And God's

Let us fix our eyes on Jesus, the author and
perfecter of our faith, who for the joy set before him
endured the cross, scorning its shame, and sat down
at the right hand of the throne of God.

Hebrews 12:2 NIV

The words are as familiar as they are true: "First things first." But sometimes, in the busy world in which we live, placing first things first can be difficult indeed. Why? Because so many people are expecting so many things from us! We have families to care for, students to teach, administrators to please, and bills to pay. What's a teacher to do? The answer to that question is straightforward: we must let God handle it.

This morning, and every morning after this one, start your day with time of prayer and consultation with the Giver of all things good. Prioritize your day according to God's commandments; seek His will first, and trust His wisdom. Then, you can face the day with the assurance that the same God who created our universe out of nothingness can help you place first things first in your own life.

The things that matter most in this world
can never be held in your hand.

Gloria Gaither

If you've found yourself breathlessly chasing
the guy in front of you, break free. Spend
some time with your family. Take a walk with
someone you love. Hold a three-year-old
on your lap and tell him or her a story.
Life is simply too short to be spent
plodding around in endless circles.

James Dobson

He is no fool who gives what he cannot
keep to gain what he cannot lose.

Jim Elliot

Blessed are those who know what on earth
they are here on earth to do and set themselves
about the business of doing it.

Max Lucado

The thing you should want most is God's kingdom and doing what God wants. Then all these other things you need will be given to you.

Matthew 6:33 NCV

A Prayer for Today

Lord, let Your priorities be my priorities.
Let Your will be my will. Let Your Word
be my guide, and let me grow in faith and
in wisdom this day and every day.

Amen

CHAPTER 26

This Is the Day

This is the day which the LORD has made;
let us rejoice and be glad in it.

Psalm 118:24 NASB

The familiar words of Psalm 118 remind us that today, like every day, is a priceless gift from God. And as teachers, we are doubly blessed: we can celebrate the glory of God's creation, and we can celebrate the precious students that He has entrusted to our care.

What do you expect from the day ahead? Are you expecting God to do wonderful things, or are you living beneath a cloud of apprehension and doubt? Do you expect God to use you in unexpected ways, or do you expect another uneventful day to pass with little fanfare? As a thoughtful believer, the answer to these questions should be obvious.

For Christian believers, every new day offers exciting possibilities. God's Word promises that Christ has come to this earth to give us abundant life and eternal salvation. We, in turn, should respond to God's gifts by treasuring each day and using our time here on earth to glorify our Creator and share the Good News of His Son.

Each day is a special gift from God, a treasure to be savored and celebrated. May we—as believers who have so much to celebrate—never fail to praise our Creator by rejoicing in His glorious creation.

If you're a thinking Christian,
you will be a joyful Christian.

Marie T. Freeman

God knows everything.
He can manage everything, and He loves us.
Surely this is enough for a fullness of joy
that is beyond words.

Hannah Whitall Smith

The one word in the spiritual vocabulary is now.

Oswald Chambers

Enjoy this day . . . compliments of God.

Anonymous

May the God of hope fill you with all joy and peace as you trust in him, so that you may overflow with hope by the power of the Holy Spirit.

Romans 15:13 NIV

A Prayer for Today

Dear Lord, You have given me so many blessings; let me celebrate Your gifts. Make me thankful, loving, responsible, and wise. I praise You, Father, for the gift of Your Son and for the priceless gift of salvation. Make me a joyful Christian, a worthy example to others, and a dutiful servant to You this day and forever.

Amen

CHAPTER 27

Finding Mentors . . .
and Becoming One

A wise man will hear and increase in learning,
and a man of understanding will
acquire wise counsel.

Proverbs 1:5 NASB

Do you wish to become a better teacher and a wiser person? Then you must walk with people who, by their words and their presence, make you wiser. But that's not all; you must *avoid* those people who encourage you to think foolish thoughts or do foolish things.

Today, as a gift to yourself, select, from your friends and co-workers, a mentor whose judgement you trust. Then listen carefully to your mentor's advice and be willing to accept that advice, *even* if accepting it requires effort or pain or both. Consider your mentor to be God's gift to you. Thank God for that gift, and treasure the wisdom that you gain.

And what should you do with all that hard-earned knowledge that you acquire from your mentor? Share it, of course, with the students and co-workers who are wise enough to learn *from you*.

God often keeps us on the path by
guiding us through the counsel of friends and
trusted spiritual advisors.

Bill Hybels

Yes, the Spirit was sent to be our Counselor.
Yes, Jesus speaks to us personally.
But often he works through
another human being.

John Eldredge

God guides through the counsel of good people.

E. Stanley Jones

It takes a wise person to give good advice,
but an even wiser person to take it.

Marie T. Freeman

Choose my instruction instead of silver,
knowledge rather than choice gold,
for wisdom is more precious than rubies,
and nothing you desire can compare with her.

Proverbs 8:10-11 NIV

A Prayer for Today

Dear Lord, thank You for family members,
for friends, and for mentors. When I am
troubled, let me turn to them for help,
for guidance, for comfort, and for perspective.
And Father, let me be a friend and mentor
to others—especially to my students—
so that my love for You may be reflected
in my genuine concern for them.

Amen

CHAPTER 28

Finding Purpose in the Classroom and Beyond

*And we know that all things work together for good
to those who love God, to those who are
the called according to His purpose.*

Romans 8:28 NKJV

The messages that we teach and the lives that we lead can have a profound impact upon our students. All of us remember teachers who greatly influenced our own lives. Now, it's our turn.

In the classroom, our purpose is clear: we must ensure that the messages we share with our students are sound, practical, and true. The ultimate truth, of course, is found in the Word of God through the person of His Son, Jesus. And even if Bible teachings are not a formal part of a school's curriculum, God's Word should be firmly planted in the heart of every Christian who teaches there.

Our students need encouraging mentors and worthy role models. As we stand before our students each day, we teach "what we know" and "who we are." And make no mistake: our students will see us for who we really are and what we really believe. Let us teach—and live—accordingly.

His life is our light—our purpose
and meaning and reason for living.

Anne Graham Lotz

The born-again Christian sees life not as
a blurred, confused, meaningless mass,
but as something planned and purposeful.

Billy Graham

The Christian life is not simply following
principles but being empowered to fulfill
our purpose: knowing and exalting Christ.

Franklin Graham

You cannot be the person God meant you to be,
and you cannot live the life he meant you to
live, unless you live from the heart.

John Eldredge

God chose you to be his people,
so I urge you now to live the life
to which God called you.

❧

Ephesians 4:1 NCV

A Prayer for Today

Dear Lord, I seek to live a meaningful life;
I will turn to You to find that meaning.
I will study Your Word, I will obey
Your commandments, I will trust
Your providence, and I will honor Your Son.
Give me Your blessings, Father, and lead me
along a path that is pleasing to You,
today, tomorrow, and forever.

❧

Amen

My Thoughts & Prayers
from This Week

_____

_____

_____

_____

_____

_____

_____

_____

_____

_____

_____

_____

_____

_____

_____

_____

_____

_____

_____

_____

_____

_____

_____

_____

My Thoughts & Prayers
for Next Week

CHAPTER 29

The Lessons We Really Teach

Be an example to the believers in word, in conduct,
in love, in spirit, in faith, in purity.
1 Timothy 4:12 NKJV

We teach our students by the words we speak and the lives we lead, but not necessarily in that order. Sometimes, our actions speak so loudly that they drown out our words completely. That's why, as teachers, we must make certain that the lives we lead are in harmony with the lessons we preach.

An important part of God's plan for your life is found in the example that you set for your students. Are you the kind of teacher whose life serves as a memorable model of righteousness and godliness? If so, you are a powerful force for good in your classroom and in your world.

Phillips Brooks advised, "Be such a man, and live such a life, that if every man were such as you, and every life a life like yours, this earth would be God's Paradise." And that's sound advice because our families and our students are watching . . . and so, for that matter, is God.

As we live moment by moment under
the control of the Spirit, His character,
which is the character of Jesus, becomes evident
to those around us.

Anne Graham Lotz

Among the most joyful people I have known
have been some who seem to have had
no human reason for joy. The sweet fragrance
of Christ has shown through their lives.

Elisabeth Elliot

For one man who can introduce another to
Jesus Christ by the way he lives and by
the atmosphere of his life, there are a thousand
who can only talk jargon about him.

Oswald Chambers

There is nothing anybody else can do that
can stop God from using us . . .
We can turn everything into a testimony.

Corrie ten Boom

> *By this we know that we have*
> *come to know Him,*
> *if we keep His commandments.*
>
> ❧
>
> 1 John 2:3 NASB

A Prayer for Today

Dear Lord, because I am a teacher,
I am an example to my students.
Let me be a worthy example, Father,
so that my words and my deeds
may be a tribute to You.

❧

Amen

CHAPTER 30

Following in His Footsteps

If anyone serves Me, let him follow Me;
and where I am, there My servant will be also.
If anyone serves Me, him My Father will honor.

John 12:26 NKJV

Each day, as we awaken from sleep, we are confronted with countless opportunities to serve God and to follow in the footsteps of His Son. When we do, our Heavenly Father guides our steps and blesses our endeavors.

As citizens of a fast-changing world, we face challenges that sometimes leave us feeling overworked, overcommitted, and overwhelmed. But God has different plans for us. He intends that we slow down long enough to praise Him and to glorify His Son. When we do, He lifts our spirits and enriches our lives.

Today provides a glorious opportunity to place yourself in the service of the One who is the Giver of all blessings. May you seek His will, may you trust His word, and may you walk in the footsteps of His Son.

Christ is like a river that is continually flowing.
There are always fresh supplies of water coming
from the fountain-head, so that a man may live
by it and be supplied with water all his life.
So Christ is an ever-flowing fountain;
he is continually supplying his people,
and the fountain is not spent. They who live
upon Christ may have fresh supplies from him
for all eternity; they may have an increase of
blessedness that is new, and new still,
and which never will come to an end.

Jonathan Edwards

Lord, I am no longer my own, but Yours. Put me
to what You will, rank me with whom You will.
Let me be employed by You or laid aside for
You, exalted for You or brought low by You.
Let me have all things, let me have nothing.
I freely and heartily yield all things to Your
pleasure and disposal. And now, O glorious and
blessed God, Father, Son, and Holy Spirit,
You are mine and I am Yours. So be it. Amen.

John Wesley

*Anyone who does not take his cross and
follow me is not worthy of me.
Whoever finds his life will lose it and
whoever loses his life for my sake will find it.*

❧

Matthew 10:38-39 NIV

A Prayer for Today

Dear Lord, You sent Your Son so that
I might have abundant life and eternal life.
Thank You, Father, for my Savior, Christ Jesus.
I will follow Him, honor Him, and share
His Good News, this day and every day.

❧

Amen

CHAPTER 31

God's Calling

But as God has distributed to each one,
as the Lord has called each one, so let him walk.
1 Corinthians 7:17 NKJV

God is calling you to fulfill an important role in His kingdom, and it is vitally important that you heed that calling. God's purpose for your life unfolds day by day. Each new morning offers fresh opportunities to study God's Word and seek His will. That's why it is imperative that you take time for a daily conference with your Heavenly Father. No habit is more important to your spiritual health than the discipline of daily prayer and devotion to your Creator.

Because you are a teacher, you have a *special* calling: a mission to help shape minds and mold lives. And make no mistake: your mission is near and dear to God's heart. Both inside and outside the classroom, there remains much work to be done . . . and the time to begin that work is now.

If God has called you, do not spend time
looking over your shoulder to see
who is following you.

Corrie ten Boom

I've never met anyone who became instantly
mature. It's a painstaking process that God
takes us through, and it includes such things
as waiting, failing, losing, and
being misunderstood—each calling
for extra doses of perseverance.

Charles Swindoll

Oh, that we might discern the will of God,
surrender to His calling, resign the masses
of activities, and do a few things well.
What a legacy that would be for our children.

Beth Moore

Jesus is calling the weary to rest,
Calling today, calling today,
Bring Him your burden and you shall be blest;
He will not turn you away.

Fanny Crosby

So the last shall be first, and the first last: for many be called, but few chosen.

Matthew 20:16 KJV

A Prayer for Today

Heavenly Father, You have called me to teach, and I acknowledge that calling. In these quiet moments before this busy day unfolds, I come to You. I will study Your Word and seek Your guidance. Give me the wisdom to know Your will for my life and the courage to follow wherever You may lead me, today and forever.

Amen

My Thoughts & Prayers
for the Month

My Thoughts & Prayers
for the Month

Bible Verses to Consider

Encouragement

Shepherd the flock of God which is among you.

1 Peter 5:2 NKJV

*Finally, all of you be of one mind,
having compassion for one another;
love as brothers, be tenderhearted, be courteous.*

1 Peter 3:8 NKJV

*When you talk, do not say harmful things,
but say what people need—words that will help
others become stronger. Then what you say
will do good to those who listen to you.*

Ephesians 4:29 NCV

*But encourage each other daily,
while it is still called today, so that none of you
is hardened by sin's deception.*

Hebrews 3:13 HCSB

Reckless words pierce like a sword,
but the tongue of the wise
brings healing.

Proverbs 12:18 NIV

Faith

*The Good News shows how God makes people
right with himself—that it begins
and ends with faith. As the Scripture says,
"But those who are right with God
will live by trusting in him."*

Romans 1:17 NCV

*But he must ask in faith without any doubting,
for the one who doubts is like the surf of the sea,
driven and tossed by the wind.*

James 1:6 NASB

*Now without faith it is impossible to please God,
for the one who draws near to Him
must believe that He exists
and rewards those who seek Him.*

Hebrews 11:6 HCSB

The righteous

will live by his faith.

Habakkuk 2:4 NIV

Kindness

Be kind to one another, tender-hearted,
forgiving each other, just as God in Christ
also has forgiven you.

Ephesians 4:32 NASB

Be kindly affectionate to one another with brotherly
love, in honor giving preference to one another;
not lagging in diligence, fervent in spirit, serving
the Lord; rejoicing in hope, patient in tribulation,
continuing steadfastly in prayer.

Romans 12:10-12 NKJV

So in everything, do to others what you
would have them do to you,
for this sums up the Law and the Prophets.

Matthew 7:12 NIV

Assuredly, I say to you, inasmuch as you did it
to one of the least of these My brethren,
you did it to Me.

Matthew 25:40 NKJV

Carry each other's burdens,
and in this way you will fulfill
the law of Christ.

Galatians 6:2 NIV

Wisdom

But the wisdom that is from above is first pure,
then peaceable, gentle, willing to yield,
full of mercy and good fruits,
without partiality and without hypocrisy.

James 3:17 NKJV

Do not deceive yourselves. If any one of you thinks
he is wise by the standards of this age, he should
become a "fool" so that he may become wise.
For the wisdom of this world
is foolishness in God's sight.

1 Corinthians 3:18-19 NIV

Trust in the LORD with all thine heart;
and lean not unto thine own understanding.
In all thy ways acknowledge him,
and he shall direct thy paths.

Proverbs 3:5-6 KJV

Those who are wise will shine like the brightness of
the heavens, and those who lead many
to righteousness, like the stars for ever and ever.

Daniel 12:3 NIV

Happy is the man
who finds wisdom,
and the man who
gains understanding.

Proverbs 3:13 NKJV

God's Love

And we have known and believed the love that
God has for us. God is love, and he who abides in
love abides in God, and God in him.

1 John 4:16 NKJV

The unfailing love of the LORD never ends!

Lamentations 3:22 NLT

Praise the LORD, all you nations. For he loves us
with unfailing love; the faithfulness of the LORD
endures forever. Praise the LORD!

Psalm 117 NLT

For God so loved the world, that he gave his only
begotten Son, that whosoever believeth in him
should not perish, but have everlasting life.

John 3:16 KJV

The Lord is full of compassion and mercy.

James 5:11 NIV